God's Word For Today's World

Langham

PREACHING RESOURCES

God's Word For Today's World

John R. W. Stott

Langham

PREACHING RESOURCES

© 2015 by The Literary Executors of John R. W. Stott

Published 2015 by Langham Preaching Resources
an imprint of Langham Publishing
www.langhampublishing.org

Langham Publishing and its imprints are a ministry of Langham Partnership

Langham Partnership
PO Box 296, Carlisle, Cumbria CA3 9WZ, UK
www.langham.org

ISBNs:
978-1-78368-937-8 Print
978-1-78368-935-4 Mobi
978-1-78368-936-1 ePub
978-178-368-912-5 PDF

First published in 1982 by InterVarsity Press as *The Bible: Book for Today*, updated in 2015 by
Langham Publishing.

John R. W. Stott has asserted his right under the Copyright, Designs and Patents Act, 1988 to be
identified as the Author of this work.

British Library Cataloguing in Publication Data
Langham Preaching Resources
Stott, John R. W. author.
God's word for today's world.
1. Christian life--Biblical teaching. 2. Bible--
Evidences, authority, etc.
I. Title
230-dc23

ISBN-13: 9781783689378

Cover & Book Design: projectluz.com

Contents

Foreword

John Stott was known for his remarkable capacity to explain the Bible clearly and relevantly. Thousands across the world have expressed gratitude for the way he introduced them to the dynamic power of the Bible. More than that, his books and his preaching became famous for their bridge-building between the Scriptures and the contemporary world: he was concerned to listen carefully to both worlds, and to ensure that that vital connection was made.

Originally published under the title *The Bible: Book for Today*, this booklet reflects Stott's concern that the Scriptures should be taken seriously in every age and every culture. The material was first delivered as a series of five sermons in All Souls Church, London, during February and March 1980, so each chapter seeks to expound a biblical text.

It has been revised and updated by Catherine Nicholson, but its essential content remains the same as when it was first published over 30 years ago. Stott addresses themes that are as important today as they were then. As he wrote in the original preface, 'This is a basic book about the historic Christian attitude to Scripture, and about the Bible's own understanding of itself, which need to be re-stated in every generation, and which remain the essential perspective from which to grapple with other pressing problems.' It is the privilege of Langham Preaching Resources to make this title available to a new generation of readers around the world.

Catherine Nicholson & Jonathan Lamb

April 2014

Introduction

L et me make a few points as we start.

First, the Bible continues to be a world bestseller. Why? The complete Bible has been translated into over 500 languages, with the New Testament available in nearly 1300 languages. Some estimates suggest that over 5 billion copies of the Bible have been printed. Why does this old book remain at the top of the charts?

Second, and paradoxically, this much-*purchased* book is a much-*neglected* book. Probably tens of thousands of people who buy the Bible never read it. Even in churches, knowledge of the Bible is very poor. Over 60 years ago Cyril Garbett, the then Archbishop of York, wrote that, 'the majority of men and women (in England) neither say their prayers, except in some terrifying emergency, nor read their Bibles, unless to look for help in a crossword puzzle, nor enter a church from one end of the year to the other, except for a baptism, a marriage or a funeral'. And if that was true 60 years ago, it is even more true today.

- Few parents read the Bible to their children, let alone teach them out of it;
- Few church members make a practice of daily Bible meditation;
- Few preachers wrestle conscientiously with the biblical text so as to grasp both its original meaning and its application today;
- Some church leaders are brash enough publicly to express their disagreement with its plain doctrinal or ethical teaching.

It is a tragic situation. What can be done to remedy it?

My third introductory point concerns the conviction that the Bible is a book, indeed *the* book, for today. It is God's Word for today's world. Until quite recently, all Christian churches have recognised its unique inspiration and consequent authority. Certainly, submission to the authority of Scripture (or, as I think we should express it better, submission to the authority of God as it is mediated to us through Scripture), has always been, and still remains, a major hallmark of evangelical Christians. We believe its instruction. We embrace its promises. We seek to obey its commands. Why? Mainly because we believe the Bible is the Word of God, but also because he speaks to us through it with a living voice. The Bible was the book for yesterday. Without doubt it will be the book for tomorrow. But for us it is the book for today.

So then, its continuing popularity, its regrettable neglect and its contemporary relevance are three good reasons why we should give our minds to *God's Word for today's world*.

1

God and the Bible

Our first topic, 'God and the Bible', introduces us to the subject of revelation. For this I ask you to turn to my text, which is Isaiah 55:8–11. God himself is speaking:

> 'For my thoughts are not your thoughts,
>   neither are your ways my ways', declares the LORD.
> 'As the heavens are higher than the earth,
>   so are my ways higher than your ways
>   and my thoughts than your thoughts.
> As the rain and the snow
>   come down from heaven,
> and do not return to it
>   without watering the earth
> and making it bud and flourish,
>   so it yields seed for the sower and bread for the eater,
> so is my word that goes out from my mouth:
>   it will not return to me empty,
> but will accomplish what I desire
>   and achieve the purpose for which I sent it.'

From this great text there are at least three important lessons to learn.

The reasonableness of revelation: Why does God need to speak?

Some people find the very concept of revelation difficult. The idea that God should disclose himself to mankind seems impossible. 'Why should he?' they ask, 'and how could he?' But we obviously need God to reveal himself. We cannot understand God unless he reveals himself. Most people in every age have felt baffled by the mysteries of human life and human experience. So most people have admitted that they need wisdom from outside themselves if they are ever to fathom the meaning of their own being, let alone the meaning of the being of God, if indeed there is a God. Let me take you right back to Plato, a philosopher in classical Greece. He speaks in the Phaedo about our having to sail the seas of darkness and doubt on the little 'raft' of our own understanding, 'not without risk', he adds, 'as I admit, if a man cannot find some word of God which will more surely and safely carry him'.

Without revelation, without divine instruction and direction, we human beings feel ourselves to be like a boat drifting rudderless on the high seas; like a leaf that is being tossed helplessly by the wind; like a blind person groping in the darkness. How can we find our way? More important, how can we find God's way without his direction? Verses 8 and 9 tell us that it is impossible for humans to discover God simply by their own intelligence: 'My thoughts are not your thoughts, neither are your ways my ways, declares the Lord. As the heavens are higher than the earth, so are my ways higher than your ways and my thoughts than your thoughts.' In other words, there is a great gap fixed between God's mind and human minds. The text shows a contrast between the ways and the thoughts of God on the one hand, and the ways and the thoughts of human beings on the other. That is, between what *we* think and do, and what *God* thinks and does, there is this great chasm. The thoughts and ways of God are as much higher than the thoughts and ways of man as the heavens are higher than the earth: that means infinity.

> How can we find God's way without his direction?

Consider God's thoughts. How can we discover his thoughts or read his mind? We can't even read each other's thoughts. We try to. We look into each other's faces to see if they are smiling or frowning. We peer into each other's eyes to see whether they are flashing or twinkling or serious or bright. But it is a risky business. If I stood here in the pulpit silent, and maintained a straight face, you wouldn't have the first idea what I was thinking about. Try. Let me stop talking for a few moments. Now, what was going on in my mind? Any guesses? No? Well, I'll tell you. I was scaling the steeple of All Souls Church, trying to reach the top! But you didn't know. You hadn't the faintest notion what I was thinking. Of course not. You can't read my mind. If we are silent, it is impossible to read one another's minds.

How much less possible is it to penetrate into the thoughts of Almighty God? His mind is infinite. His thoughts tower above our thoughts as the heavens tower above the earth. It is ridiculous to suppose that we could ever penetrate into the mind of God. There is no ladder by which our little mind can climb up into his infinite mind. There is no bridge that we can throw across the chasm of infinity. There is no way to reach or to fathom God.

So it is only reasonable to say that unless God takes the initiative to disclose what is in his mind, we shall never be able to find out. Unless God makes himself known to us, we can never know him, and all the world's altars – like the one Paul saw in Athens – will bear the tragic inscription, 'TO AN UNKNOWN GOD' (Acts 17:23).

This is the place to begin our study. It is the place of humility before the infinite God. It is also the place of wisdom, as we see the reasonableness of the idea of revelation.

The way of revelation: How has God spoken?

Realising that we need God to reveal himself, how has he done so? In principle, in the same way that we reveal or disclose ourselves to one another, that is, by both *works* and *words*, by things we do and say.

a) Works

Creative art has always been one of the main means of human self-expression. We know that there is something inside us which has to come out, and we struggle to bring it to birth. Some people make music or write poetry; others use one of the visual arts – drawing, painting or photography, pottery, sculpture, carving or architecture, dance or drama. It is interesting that of these artistic media, pottery is the one most frequently used of God in Scripture – presumably because the potter was a well-known figure in the villages of Palestine. So God is said to have 'formed' or 'fashioned' the earth, and mankind to dwell upon it (e.g. Gen 2:7; Ps 8:3; Jer 32:17).

Moreover, he himself is seen in his works. 'The heavens declare the glory of God and the whole earth is full of his glory' (Ps 19:1; Isa 6:3). Or, as Paul writes near the beginning of Romans, 'what may be known about God is plain to them (the Gentile world), because God has made it plain to them. For since the creation of the world God's invisible qualities – his eternal power and divine nature – have been clearly seen, being understood from what has been made, so that people are without excuse' (Rom 1:19–20). In other words, just as human artists reveal themselves in their painting, sculpture or music, so the divine artist has revealed himself in the beauty, balance, intricacy and order of his creation. From it we learn something of his wisdom, power and faithfulness. This is usually referred to as 'natural' revelation, because it has been given in and through 'nature'.

b) Words

It is not to works that Isaiah 55 refers, however, but rather to the second and more direct way in which we make ourselves known to one another, and God has made himself known to us, namely through *words*. Speech is the fullest and most flexible means of communication between two human beings. I mentioned earlier that if I remained silent and straight-faced in the pulpit, you could not discover what was going on in my mind. But now the situation has changed. Now you do know what is going on in my mind, because I am no longer silent. I am speaking. I am clothing the thoughts of my mind in the words of my mouth. The words of my mouth are putting across to you the thoughts of my mind.

Speech, then, is the best means of communication, and speech is the main model used in the Bible to illustrate God's self-revelation. Look back at my text and read verses 10 and 11: 'As the rain and the snow come down from heaven, and do not return to it without watering the earth and making it bud and flourish, so that it yields seed for the sower and bread for the eater, so is my word . . . ' Notice the second reference to heaven and earth: it is because the heavens are higher than the earth that the rain comes down from heaven to water the earth. Notice also that the writer goes straight from the thoughts in the mind of God to the words in the mouth of God: 'So is my word that goes out from my mouth; it will not return to me empty, but will accomplish what I desire and achieve the purpose for which I sent it.' The parallel is plain. As the heavens are higher than the earth, but the rain comes down from heaven to water the earth, so God's thoughts are higher than our thoughts, but they come down to us, because his word goes forth from his mouth and thus conveys his thoughts to us. As the prophet has said earlier, 'for the mouth of the Lord has spoken' (Isa 40:5). He was referring to one of his own oracles, but he described it as a message coming out of the mouth of God. Or as Paul wrote in 2 Timothy, 'all Scripture is God-breathed'. That is, Scripture is God's Word, coming from God's mouth.

Having said this, it is important for me to add a couple of qualifications in order to clarify our understanding of how God spoke his Word.

> Scripture is God's Word, coming from God's mouth

First, *God's Word* (now recorded in Scripture) *was closely related to his activity.* Put differently, he spoke to his people by deeds as well as words. He made himself known to Israel in their history, and so directed its development as to bring to them both his salvation and his judgment. So, he rescued the people from their slavery in Egypt:

- he brought them safely across the desert, and settled them in the promised land;
- he preserved their national identity through the period of the judges;
- he gave them kings to rule over them, despite the fact that their demand for a human king was in part a rejection of his own kingship;
- his judgment fell upon them for their persistent disobedience when they were deported into Babylonian exile;
- he restored them to their own land and enabled them to rebuild their nationhood and their temple.

Above all, for us sinners and for our salvation, he sent his eternal Son, Jesus Christ, to be born, to live and work, to suffer and die, to rise and to pour out the Holy Spirit. Through these deeds, first in the Old Testament story but supremely in Jesus Christ, God was actively and personally revealing himself.

For this reason it has been fashionable for some theologians to distinguish sharply between 'personal' revelation (through God's deeds) and 'propositional' revelation (through his words), and then to reject his words in favour of his deeds. This polarisation is unnecessary. There is no need for us to choose between these two types of revelation. God used them both. Moreover, they were closely related to one another, for God's words interpreted his deeds. He raised up the prophets to explain what he was doing to Israel, and he raised up the apostles to explain what he was doing through Christ. It is true that the climax of his revelation of himself was the person of Jesus. He was God's Word made flesh. He showed forth the glory of God. To have seen him was to have seen the Father (see John 1:14, 18, 14:9). Nevertheless, this historical and personal revelation would not have benefited us unless, along with it, God had shown us the significance of the person and work of his Son.

We must, then, avoid the trap of setting 'personal' and 'propositional' revelation over against each other as alternatives. It is more accurate to say that God has revealed himself in Christ and in the biblical witness to Christ. Neither is complete without the other.

Second, *God's Word has come to us through human words.* When God spoke, he didn't audibly shout to people out of a clear blue sky. No, he spoke through prophets (in the Old Testament) and through apostles (in the New Testament). They were real people. Divine inspiration was not a mechanical process which reduced the human authors of the Bible to machines. Divine inspiration was a personal process in which the human authors of the Bible were usually in full possession of their faculties. We have only to read the Bible in order to see that this is so. The writers of narrative (and there is a great deal of historical narrative in the Bible, Old and New Testament alike) used historical records. Some are quoted in the Old Testament. Luke tells us at the beginning of his gospel of his own painstaking historical research. Next, all the biblical authors developed their own distinctive literary styles and theological emphases. So Scripture is richly diverse. Nevertheless, through their varied approaches God himself was speaking.

This truth of the double authorship of the Bible (namely that it is the Word of God *and* the words of men, or more strictly the Word of God *through* the words of men) is the Bible's own account of itself. The Old Testament law, for example, is sometimes called 'the law of Moses' and sometimes 'the law of God' or 'the law of the Lord'. In Hebrews 1:1 we read that God spoke to the fathers through the prophets. In 2 Peter 1:21, however, we read that men spoke from God as they were moved by the Holy Spirit. So God spoke and men spoke. They spoke *from* him, and he spoke *through* them. Both these things are true.

Further, we must hold them together. As in the incarnate Word (Jesus Christ), so in the written Word (the Bible), the divine and human elements combine and do not contradict one another. This analogy, which was developed quite early in the history of the church, is often criticised today. And obviously it is not exact, since Jesus was a person, whereas the Bible is a book. Nevertheless, the analogy remains helpful, provided that we remember its limitations. For example, we must never affirm the deity of Jesus in such a way as to deny his humanity, nor affirm his humanity in such a way as to deny his deity. So it is with the Bible. On the one hand, the Bible is the Word of God. God spoke, deciding himself what he intended to say, yet not in such a way as to distort the personality of the human authors. On the other hand, the Bible is the word of men. Men spoke, using their faculties freely, yet not in such a way as to distort the truth of the divine message.

The double authorship of the Bible will affect the way in which we read it. Because it is the word of men, we shall study it like every other book, using our minds, investigating its words and meaning, its historical origins and its literary composition. But because it is also the Word of God, we shall study it like no other book, on our knees, humbly, crying to God for illumination and for the ministry of the Holy Spirit, without whom we can never understand his Word.

The purpose of revelation: Why did God speak?

We have considered *how* God spoke: now, *why* did he speak? The answer is not just to teach us, but also to save us; not just to instruct us, but specifically to instruct us 'for salvation' (2 Tim 3:15). The Bible has this severely practical purpose.

Returning to Isaiah 55, this is the emphasis of verses 10 and 11. The rain and the snow come down to us from heaven and do not return there. They accomplish a purpose on earth. They water it. They cause it to bud and flourish. They make it fruitful. In the same way, God's Word, issuing from his mouth and disclosing his mind, does not return to him empty. It accomplishes a purpose. And God's purpose in sending rain to the earth and his purpose in speaking his Word to human beings are similar. In both cases it is fruitfulness. His rain makes the earth fruitful; his Word makes human lives fruitful. It saves them, changing them into the likeness of Jesus Christ. Salvation is certainly the context. For in verses 6 and 7 the prophet has spoken of God's mercy and pardon, and in verse 12 he will go on to speak of the joy and peace of God's redeemed people.

> His rain makes the earth fruitful; his Word makes human lives fruitful

In fact, here lies the main difference between God's revelation in creation ('natural', because given in nature, and 'general', because given to all mankind) and his revelation in the Bible ('supernatural', because given by inspiration, and 'special', because given to and through particular people). Through the created universe God reveals his glory, power and faithfulness, but not the way of salvation. If we want to learn his gracious plan to save sinners, we must turn to the Bible, for it is there that he speaks to us of Christ.

Conclusion

From our text in Isaiah 55 we have learned three truths:

- First, divine revelation is not only reasonable, but also indispensable. Without it we could never know God.
- Second, divine revelation is through words. God spoke through human words and in doing so was explaining his deeds.
- Third, divine revelation is for salvation. It points us to Christ as Saviour.

My conclusion is very simple. It is a call to humility. Nothing is more hostile to spiritual growth than arrogance, and nothing is more vital for growth than humility. We need to humble ourselves before the infinite God, acknowledging the limitations of our human mind (that we could never find him by ourselves), and acknowledging our own sinfulness (that we could never reach him by ourselves).

Jesus called this the humility of a little child. God hides himself from the wise and clever, he said, but reveals himself to 'little children' (Matt 11:25). He was not belittling our minds, for God has given them to us. Rather he was showing how we are to use them. The true function of the mind is not to stand in judgment on God's Word, but to sit in humility under it, eager to hear it, grasp it, apply it and obey it in the practicalities of daily living.

The 'humility' of children is seen not only in the way they learn, but also in the way they receive. Children are dependants. None of their possessions has been earned. All they have has been given to them freely. Like children, then, we are to 'receive the kingdom of God' (Mark 10:15). For sinners do not deserve, and cannot earn, eternal life (which is the life of God's kingdom); we have to humble ourselves to receive it as the free gift of God.

2

Christt and the Bible

Our first topic was 'God and the Bible'. We considered the origin of Scripture, where it came from – the great subject of revelation. Our second topic is 'Christ and the Bible': we shall be thinking now not of its origin but of its *purpose*; not where has it come from, but what has it been given for? Our text is John 5:31–40. Jesus is speaking to his Jewish contemporaries and says,

> You study the Scriptures diligently because you think that in them you have eternal life. These are the very Scriptures that testify about me, yet you refuse to come to me to have life.
>
> (John 5:39–40)

From these words of Jesus we learn two significant truths about Christ and the Bible.

The Scriptures bear witness to Christ

Jesus himself says so very plainly: 'These are the very Scriptures that testify about me' (v. 39). The major function of Scripture is to bear witness to Christ.

The context of our passage is concerned with testimony to Christ: what testimony can validate the claims of Jesus of Nazareth? He himself tells us. To begin with, he does not rely on his own testimony to himself, as is clear from verse 31 – 'If I testify about myself, my testimony is not true.' Of course Jesus is not suggesting that he is telling lies about himself. Indeed, he later rejects a criticism of the Pharisees by insisting that his testimony to himself is true

(John 8:14). His point here is that self-testimony is inadequate: there would be something suspicious about it if the only testimony he had came from him alone. No, 'there is another who testifies in my favour', he says (v. 32). So the testimony he relies upon is not his own testimony. Nor is it human testimony, even the testimony of that outstanding witness, John the Baptist. 'You have sent to John, and he has testified to the truth. Not that I accept human testimony . . . ' (vv. 33–34).

So then, it isn't from me, and it isn't from human beings, says Jesus. Of course, John was 'a lamp that burned and gave light' (v. 35), and they had been willing 'to choose for a time to enjoy his light'. But the testimony that Jesus claimed was greater. It was greater than his own testimony to himself, and greater than the testimony of any human being, even of John. It was the testimony of his *Father*. 'And the Father who sent me has himself testified concerning me' (v. 37). Moreover, the Father's testimony to the Son took two forms. First, it was given through the mighty works, the miracles, which the Father enabled him to do (v. 36). But second, and more directly still, it was given through the Scriptures, which are the Father's testimony to the Son. Verses 36–39 make this plain:

> I have testimony weightier than that of John. For the works that the Father has given me to finish – the very works that I am doing – testify that the Father has sent me. And the Father who sent me has himself testified concerning me. You have never heard his voice nor seen his form, nor does his word dwell in you, for you do not believe the one he sent. You study the Scriptures diligently because you think that in them you have eternal life. These are the very Scriptures that testify about me . . .

It was the consistent teaching of Jesus that Old Testament Scripture was God's Word bearing witness to him. For example, he said, 'Abraham rejoiced at the thought of seeing my day' (John 8:56). And in John 5:46 he says, 'Moses . . . wrote about me.' Again, 'the Scriptures . . . testify about me' (v. 39). At the beginning of his ministry, when he went to worship in the synagogue at Nazareth, he read from Isaiah 61 about the Messiah's mission and message of liberation, and added: 'Today this Scripture is fulfilled in your hearing' (Luke 4:21). In other words, 'If you want to know whom the prophet was writing about, he was writing about me.' Jesus continued to say this kind of thing throughout his ministry. Even after the resurrection he had not changed his mind, for 'he explained to them what was said in all the Scriptures concerning himself' (Luke 24:27). Thus from the beginning to the end of his ministry, Jesus declared that the whole prophetic testimony of the Old Testament, in all its rich diversity, pointed to him. 'The Scriptures . . . testify about me.'

But Jesus' Jewish contemporaries missed this testimony. They were very diligent students of the Old Testament, and we have no quarrel with them over their study. 'You search the Scriptures,' Jesus said. They did. They spent hours and hours in the most careful examination of the small details of Old Testament Scripture. They used to count the number of words – even the number of letters – in every book of the Bible. They knew they had been entrusted with the very words of God (Rom 3:2). They somehow thought that an accumulation of detailed biblical knowledge would bring them into right relationship with God. 'You study the Scriptures diligently because you think in them you have eternal life.' What a strange thing that was, to imagine that the Scriptures themselves could give eternal life! The Scriptures point to Christ as the Life-giver, and urge their readers to go to him for life. But instead of going to Christ to find life, they imagined that they could find life in Scripture itself. It is somewhat like getting a prescription from the doctor and then swallowing the prescription instead of getting and taking the medicine!

Some of us make the same mistake. We have an almost superstitious attitude to Bible reading, as if it had some magical effect. But there is no magic in the Bible or in the mechanical reading of the Bible. No, the written Word points to the Living Word and says to us, 'Go to Jesus.' If we do not go to the Jesus to whom it points, we miss the whole purpose of Bible reading.

Evangelical Christians are not, or ought not to be, what we are sometimes accused of being, namely 'bibliolaters', worshippers of the Bible. No, we do not worship the Bible; we worship the Christ of the Bible. Imagine a young man who is in love. He has a girlfriend who has captured his heart. Or indeed she may be his fiancée, or his wife, and he is deeply in love with her. So he carries a photograph of his beloved in his wallet, because it reminds him of her when she is faraway. Sometimes,

> If we do not go to the Jesus to whom it points, we miss the whole purpose of Bible reading

when nobody is looking, he might even take the photograph out and give it a kiss. But kissing the photograph is a poor substitute for the real thing. And so it is with the Bible. We love it only because we love him of whom it speaks.

This is the main key to the understanding of Scripture. The Bible is God's picture of Jesus. It bears witness to him. So whenever we are reading the Bible, we must look for Christ. For example, the Old Testament law is our 'guardian' to bring us to Christ (Gal 3:24). Because it condemns us for our disobedience, it makes Christ vital for us. It drives us to him, through whom alone we may find forgiveness.

> The Bible is God's picture of Jesus

Next, the Old Testament sacrifices point to that perfect sacrifice for sin made once for all upon the cross – the sacrifice of Christ for our redemption. Another example is the teaching of the Old Testament prophets who tell of the coming of the Messiah. They speak of him as a king of David's line, during whose kingdom there will be peace, righteousness and stability. They write of him as the 'seed of Abraham', through whom all nations of the world will be blessed. They depict him as the 'suffering servant of the Lord' who will die for the sins of his people, and as 'the son of man coming in the clouds of heaven' whom all peoples will serve. All these rich images of Old Testament prophecy bear witness to Christ.

When we move into the New Testament, Jesus Christ comes even more clearly into focus. The Gospels are full of him. They speak of his birth and of his public ministry, of his words and works, of his death and resurrection, and of his ascension and gift of the Holy Spirit. The book of Acts tells us what Jesus continued to do and to teach through the apostles whom he had chosen and commissioned. The letters of the apostles set forth the glory of Jesus in his divine-human person and his saving work.

When you come to the last book of the Bible, the Revelation, it too is full of Christ. For there we see him patrolling the churches on earth, sharing God's throne in heaven, riding forth on a white horse conquering, and coming in power and glory.

The old writers used to say that, just as in England every footpath and every country lane, linking on to others, will ultimately lead you to London, so every verse and every paragraph in the Bible, linking on to others, will ultimately lead you to Christ. The Scriptures bear witness to him. That is the first truth which is very plainly taught in our passage in John 5.

Christ bears witness to the Scriptures

When Jesus spoke of the testimony of John the Baptist, he referred to it as human testimony (John 5:33–34), and added that the testimony which attested to him was 'not . . . from man'. The testimony he had was greater. It was his Father's testimony through his works (v. 36) and his word (v. 38). Here, then, is Jesus' plain statement that the Old Testament Scriptures are his Father's 'word', and that this biblical testimony was not human, but divine.

This too was Jesus' consistent teaching. In fact, the major reason why we desire to submit to the authority of the Bible is that Jesus Christ authenticated it as possessing the authority of God. If we are to understand this point (which we must), then we need to distinguish between the Old and the New Testaments. The Bible, of course, is made up of them both, but Jesus was born and lived and died in the middle, between them. As a consequence, the way in which he authenticated the one is different from the way in which he authenticated the other. He looked back to the Old Testament, he looked on to the New Testament, but he authenticated them both.

a) Jesus endorsed the Old Testament

He not only described it as his Father's 'word' and 'witness', as we have seen, but he also said 'Scripture cannot be set aside' (John 10:35). At the beginning of the Sermon on the Mount he declared: 'Do not think that I have come to abolish the Law or the Prophets; I have come not to abolish them but to fulfil them. For truly I tell you, until heaven and earth disappear, not the smallest letter, not the least stroke of a pen, will by any means disappear from the law until everything is accomplished' (Matt 5:17–18). His personal attitude to the Old Testament Scriptures was one of reverent submission, for he believed that in submitting to the written Word, he was submitting to his Father's Word. Since he believed that it was from God, he interpreted his own mission as Messiah in the light of its prophetic testimony and added that certain things must come to pass, because the Scripture must be fulfilled.

Further, Jesus obeyed the moral commands of the Old Testament, as when in the temptations in the Judean wilderness he commanded the devil to leave him because of what stood written in Scripture. However subtle Satan's temptations might be, Jesus was prepared neither to listen nor to negotiate. He was determined to obey God, not the devil, and what stood written in Scripture settled the issue for him (e.g. Luke 4:4, 8, 12).

Jesus also made the Scripture his ground of appeal in all his arguments with the religious leaders of his day. He was often engaged in controversy, and on every occasion he appealed to the Scriptures. He criticised the Pharisees for adding their traditions to the Scriptures, and the Sadducees for subtracting the supernatural (e.g. the resurrection) from the Scriptures. Thus Jesus exalted Scripture as his Father's Word, to be both believed and obeyed. He permitted no changes to it, either by addition or by subtraction.

Of course he declared that, with him, the time of 'fulfilment' had come (e.g. Mark 1:14–15), and that therefore the time of waiting was over. This meant, as his followers soon recognised, that Gentiles were to be admitted to God's kingdom on equal terms with Jews, and that the Jewish ceremonial system had been made unnecessary, including its dietary laws (Mark 7:19) and – above all – its blood sacrifices.

But there is no example in the Gospels of Jesus disagreeing with the doctrinal or ethical teaching of the Old Testament. What he contradicted was the scribal misinterpretations and distortions of the Old Testament. This was his point in the Sermon on the Mount, in which six times he said in effect, 'You have heard this, but I tell you something different.' What they had 'heard' was the so-called 'traditions of the elders'. It was these which he was criticising; it was not the teaching of Moses in the law. For what stood written in Scripture he received as his Father's Word.

If this is so, and the evidence is overwhelming, we have to add that the disciple is not above his teacher. It is inconceivable that a Christian who looks to Jesus as his Teacher and Lord should have a lower view of the

> It is inconceivable that a Christian who looks to Jesus as his Teacher and Lord should have a lower view of the Old Testament than he had

Old Testament than he had. What is the sense in calling Jesus 'Teacher' and 'Lord', and then disagreeing with him? We have no liberty to disagree with him. His view of Scripture must become ours. Since he believed Scripture, so must we. Since he obeyed Scripture, so must we. He emphatically endorsed its authority.

b) Jesus made provision for the writing of the New Testament

Just as God called the prophets in the Old Testament to record and interpret what he was doing, and then 'sent' them to teach the children of Israel, so Jesus called the apostles to record and interpret what he was doing and saying, and then 'sent' them to teach the church, and indeed the world. This is the meaning of the word *apostolos,* a person 'sent' on a mission with a message. This parallel between the Old Testament prophets and the New Testament apostles was deliberate. Jesus chose twelve in order that they might be with him – to hear his words, see his works, and then bear witness out of what they had seen and heard (cf. Mark 3:14; John 15:27). Next, he promised them the Holy Spirit in order to remind them of his teaching and to supplement it, leading them into all the truth (John 14:25–26, 16:12–13). This explains why Jesus could then say to the apostles, 'Whoever listens to you listens to me; whoever rejects you rejects me' (see Matt 10:40; Luke 10:16; John 13:20). In other words, he gave them his authority, so that people's attitude to their teaching would mirror their attitude to his. Later Jesus added Paul and maybe one or two others to the apostolic band, giving them the same apostolic authority.

The apostles themselves recognised the unique authority they had been given as the teachers of the church. They did not hesitate on occasions to put themselves on a par with the Old Testament prophets, since they too were bearers of 'the word of God' (e.g. 1 Thess 2:13). They spoke and wrote in the name and with the authority of Jesus Christ. They issued commandments and expected obedience (e.g. 2 Thess 3). They even gave instructions that their letters should be read in the public assembly when Christians were gathered together for worship, therefore placing them alongside the Old Testament Scriptures (e.g. Col 4:16; 1 Thess 5:27). This is the origin of the practice, which continues to this day, of having an Old Testament and a New Testament reading in church.

A striking example of Paul's awareness of his apostolic authority occurs in his letter to the Galatians. He had climbed over the Taurus mountains on to the Galatian plateau to visit them, and had arrived a sick man. He mentions some disfigurement, which had perhaps affected his eyesight (Gal 4:13–16), and goes on to say: 'You did not treat me with contempt or scorn. Instead, you welcomed me as if I were an angel of God, as if I were Christ Jesus himself' (v. 14). Not only had they welcomed him as God's 'angel' or messenger, but they had actually listened to him as if he were Jesus Christ himself. Notice that he does not rebuke them for this. He doesn't say, 'What on earth were you thinking about, that you should have given to me the deference that you would give to Christ?' No, he applauds them for the way they had treated him. It was not merely Christian courtesy which had motivated them to welcome a stranger. It was more than that. They had recognised him as a divine messenger, an apostle, who had come to them in the name and with the authority of Christ. So they had received him as if he were Christ.

Not only did the apostles understand the teaching authority they had been given, but the early church understood it also. As soon as all the apostles had died, church leaders knew that they had moved into a new post-apostolic era. There was now no longer anybody in the church with the authority of a Paul or a Peter or a John. Bishop Ignatius of Antioch (AD 110) is perhaps the earliest clear example of this, who was ministering very soon after John, the last surviving apostle, had died. On his way to Rome to be executed, Ignatius wrote a number of letters to the Ephesians, the Romans, the Trallians and others. Several times in these he wrote: 'I do not, like Peter or Paul, issue you with commands. For I am not an apostle, but a condemned man.' Now Ignatius was a bishop in the church. But even so, he knew he was not an apostle, and he therefore did not have an apostle's authority. The early church clearly understood this difference. So, when the time came to fix the New Testament canon in the third century AD, the test of canonicity was apostolicity.

The essential questions to be asked of a disputed book were these: had it been written by an apostle? If not, did it come from the circle of the apostles? Did it contain the teaching of the apostles? Did it have the imprimatur of the apostles? If in one of these ways it could be shown to be 'apostolic', then its place in the canon of New Testament Scripture was secure.

It is extremely important to recover today this understanding of the unique authority of Christ's apostles. They were eyewitnesses of the risen Lord

(Acts 1:21–26; 1 Cor 9:1, 15:8–10), who had received a special commission and inspiration from him. We have no right, therefore, to dismiss their teaching as if it were merely their own opinions. They were not speaking or writing in their own name, but in Christ's.

Conclusion

Let me sum up. We believe the Scriptures because of Christ. He endorsed the Old Testament and he made provision for the writing of the New Testament by giving to the apostles his authority. We therefore receive the Bible from the hand of Jesus Christ. It is he who has given it his own authority. And since we are determined to submit to him, we are determined to submit to it. Our doctrine of Scripture is bound up with our loyalty to Jesus Christ. If he is our Teacher and our Lord, we have no liberty to disagree with him. Our view of Scripture must be his.

At this point some people raise an understandable objection. 'The Scriptures bear witness to Christ and Christ bears witness to the Scriptures,' they say, accurately summarising what we have been saying. 'But surely', they continue, 'this reciprocal testimony, each bearing witness to the other, is a circular argument? Does it not assume the very truth you want to prove? That is, in order to demonstrate the inspiration of Scripture you appeal to the teaching of Jesus, but you believe the teaching of Jesus only because of the inspired Scriptures. Isn't that a circular argument, and therefore invalid?'

> We therefore receive the Bible from the hand of Jesus Christ

Well, this is an important objection to face. But actually our argument has been misstated, for it is linear and not circular reasoning.

Let me put it in this way: When we first listen to the biblical witness to Christ, we read our New Testament with no preconceived doctrine of inspiration. We simply accept it as a collection of first-century historical documents, which indeed it is. Through this historical testimony, however, quite apart from any theory of biblical inspiration, the Holy Spirit brings us to faith in Jesus. Then this Jesus, in whom we have come to believe, sends us back to the Bible and gives us in his teaching a doctrine of Scripture which we did not have when we started our reading – for he now tells us that its historical testimony is also divine testimony, and that through the human agency of prophets and apostles his Father is bearing witness to him.

Whenever you read the Bible, I want to beg you to remember its major purpose. Scripture is the Father's testimony to the Son. It points to him. It says to us, 'Go to him in order to find life – abundant life – in him.' Therefore any preoccupation with the biblical text, which does not lead to a stronger commitment to Jesus Christ in faith, love, worship and obedience, is seriously perverted. It brings us under the rebuke of Jesus: 'You study the Scriptures diligently because you think that in them you have eternal life. These are the very Scriptures that testify about me, yet you refuse to come to me (to whom they bear witness) to have life.'

Scripture (as Luther used to say) is the manger or 'cradle' in which the infant Jesus lies. Don't let us inspect the cradle and forget to worship the Baby. Scripture, we might say, is the star, which still leads wise people to Jesus. Don't let us allow our astronomical curiosity so to preoccupy us that we miss the house to which it is leading, and within it the Christ-child himself. Again, we might say, Scripture is the box in which the jewel of Jesus Christ is displayed. Don't let us admire the box and overlook the jewel.

You see, it is not enough to possess a Bible, to read the Bible, love the Bible, study the Bible, know the Bible. We need to ask ourselves: *is the Christ of the Bible the centre of our lives?* If not, all our Bible reading has been futile, for this is the great purpose of the Bible.

> It is not enough to possess a Bible, to read the Bible, love the Bible, study the Bible, know the Bible. We need to ask ourselves: *is the Christ of the Bible the centre of our lives?*

3

The Holy Spirit and the Bible

All Christians know that the Holy Bible and the Holy Spirit are supposed to have something to do with each other. Indeed, all Christians believe that in some sense the Holy Bible is the creative product of the Holy Spirit. We often affirm as one of our beliefs about the Holy Spirit that 'he spoke through the prophets'. This expression echoes many similar phrases which occur in the New Testament. For example, our Lord Jesus himself once introduced a quotation from Psalm 110 with the words: 'David himself, speaking by the Holy Spirit, declared . . . ' (Mark 12:36). Similarly, the apostle Peter in his second letter wrote that 'prophets, though human, spoke from God as they were carried along by the Holy Spirit' (2 Pet 1:21) or, as the Greek verb means, they were 'carried along' by the Holy Spirit, as if by a powerful wind. There is then an important relationship between the Bible and the Spirit, which we need to investigate.

So far we have said that God is the author of the Bible, and that Jesus Christ is its main subject. Now we have to add that the Holy Spirit is its *agent*. So the Christian understanding of the Bible is essentially a Trinitarian understanding. The Bible comes from God, centres on Christ and is inspired by the Holy Spirit. So the best definition of the Bible is also Trinitarian: 'the Bible is the witness of the Father to the Son through the Holy Spirit.'

What, then, is the precise role of the Holy Spirit in the process of

> The Bible comes from God, centres on Christ and is inspired by the Holy Spirit

revelation? To answer this question we turn to the Bible itself and in particular to 1 Corinthians 2:6–16.

> We do, however, speak a message of wisdom among the mature, but not the wisdom of this age or of the rulers of this age, who are coming to nothing. No, we declare God's wisdom, a mystery that has been hidden and that God destined for our glory before time began. None of the rulers of this age understood it, for if they had, they would not have crucified the Lord of glory. However, as it is written:
>
> > 'What no eye has seen,
> >   what no ear has heard,
> >   and what no human mind has conceived' –
> >   the things God has prepared for those who love him –
>
> these are the things God has revealed to us by his Spirit.
>
> The Spirit searches all things, even the deep things of God. For who knows a person's thoughts except their own spirit within them? In the same way no one knows the thoughts of God except the Spirit of God. What we have received is not the spirit of the world, but the Spirit who is from God, so that we might understand what God has freely given us. This is what we speak, not in words taught us by human wisdom but in words taught by the Spirit, explaining spiritual realities with Spirit-taught words. The person without the Spirit does not accept the things that come from the Spirit of God but considers them foolishness, and cannot understand them because they are discerned only through the Spirit. The person with the Spirit makes judgments about all things, but such a person is not subject to merely human judgments, for, 'Who has known the mind of the Lord so as to instruct him?' But we have the mind of Christ.'

It is important that we see this text in its wider context. Up to this point in 1 Corinthians, Paul has been emphasising the 'foolishness' of the gospel. For example, 'the message of the cross is foolishness to those who are perishing' (1:18), and 'we preach Christ crucified; a stumbling-block to Jews and foolishness to Gentiles' (1:23). Or, as we might put it today, the message of the cross sounds stupid to secular intellectuals, even meaningless. So Paul now adds a corrective in case his readers should imagine that he is rejecting wisdom altogether and that he glories in folly instead. Is the apostle anti-intellectual, then? Does he scorn understanding and the use of the mind? No, certainly not.

Verses 6–7: 'We do, however, speak a message of wisdom among the mature . . . a mystery that has been hidden and that God destined for our glory before time began.' The contrasts Paul is making must not be overlooked. We do impart wisdom, he writes, but (a) only to the mature, not to non-Christians or even to very young Christians; (b) it is God's wisdom, not worldly wisdom; and (c) it is for our glorification, that is, our final perfection through sharing in God's glory, and not just to bring us to justification in Christ. We ourselves need to follow the apostle's example. In evangelising non-Christians we must concentrate on the 'foolishness' of the gospel of Christ crucified for sinners. In building up Christians into full maturity, however, we should want to lead them into an understanding of God's total purpose. Paul calls this, in verse 7, God's 'mystery that has been hidden' and in verse 9, 'the things God has prepared for those who love him'. It can be known, he stresses, only by revelation. 'The rulers of this age' (secular leaders) did not understand it, or they would never have crucified 'the Lord of glory' (v. 8). They were not exceptional, however; all human beings, if left to themselves, are ignorant of God's wisdom and purpose.

God's purpose, Paul writes here (v. 9), is something which 'no eye has seen' (it is invisible), 'no ear has heard' (it is inaudible), 'no human mind has conceived' (it is inconceivable). It is beyond the reach of human eyes, ears and minds. It is not open to scientific investigation, or even to poetic imagination. It is altogether beyond our little finite minds to work out, unless God should reveal it – which is exactly what God has done! Listen again: 'What no eye has seen, what no ear has heard, and what no human mind has conceived – the things God has prepared for those who love him' – this unimaginable splendour of his purpose – 'God has revealed to us by his Spirit'. The word 'us' is emphasised, and in the context must refer not to all of us, but to the apostle Paul who is writing, and to his fellow apostles. God gave a special revelation of these truths to special organs of revelation (the prophets in the Old Testament and the apostles in the New), and God did this 'through the Spirit'. The Holy Spirit has been the agent of this revelation.

All of this is, I'm afraid, a rather lengthy introduction to help us see the context within which Paul comes to his theme of the Holy Spirit as the agent of revelation. What he goes on to write is a marvellously comprehensive statement. He outlines the four stages of the Holy Spirit's work as agent of divine revelation.

The searching Spirit

First, the Holy Spirit is the searching Spirit (vv. 10–11). It is worth noting, just in passing, that this shows the Holy Spirit to be personal. Only persons can engage in 'search' or 'research'. To be sure, computers can undertake highly complex research of a mechanical, analytical kind. But true research involves more than collecting and analysing statistical data; it requires original thought. This, then, is work that the Holy Spirit does, because he has a mind with which he thinks. Being a divine person (and not a computer, or a vague influence or power), we need to accustom ourselves to referring to the Spirit as 'he', not 'it'.

Paul uses two fascinating little pictures to indicate the unique qualifications of the Holy Spirit in the work of revelation.

The first is that 'the Spirit searches all things, even the deep things of God' (v. 10). It is the same verb Jesus applied to the Jews 'searching the Scriptures'. The Holy Spirit is depicted as a restlessly inquisitive research worker, or even perhaps as a deep-sea diver who is seeking to fathom the deepest depths of the unfathomable being of Almighty God. For God's being is infinite in its depth, and Paul boldly declares that the Spirit of God is searching these depths. In other words, God himself is exploring the riches of his own being.

The second model or picture Paul gives is taken from human self-understanding. Verse 11: 'For who knows a person's thoughts except their own spirit within them?' 'Thoughts' is literally 'things', a human being's 'things', perhaps what we would call our 'humanness'. An ant cannot possibly conceive what it is like to be a human being. Nor can a frog, or a rabbit, or even the most intelligent ape. Nor can one human being fully understand another human being. How often we say, particularly maybe in adolescence as we are growing up, 'You just don't understand; nobody understands me.' That is true! Nobody does understand me except myself, and even my understanding of myself is limited. In the same way nobody understands you except yourself. This measure of self-understanding or self-consciousness Paul applies to the Holy Spirit: 'In the same way no one knows the thoughts of God except the Spirit of God' (v. 11). The Holy Spirit of God is here almost likened to the divine self-understanding or the divine self-consciousness. Just as nobody can understand a human being except that human being himself, so nobody can understand God except God himself. As an old hymn put it, 'God only knows the love of God'. We could equally well affirm that only God knows the wisdom of God, indeed only God knows the being of God.

So, then, the Spirit searches the depths of God, and the Spirit knows the things of God. He has an understanding of God which is unique. The question now is: What has he done with what he has searched out and come to know? Has he kept his unique knowledge to himself? No. He has done what only he is competent to do; he has revealed it. The searching Spirit became the revealing Spirit.

The revealing Spirit

What the Holy Spirit alone has come to know, he alone has made known. This has already been stated in verse 10: 'These are the things God has revealed to us [the apostles] by his Spirit'. Now Paul continues in verse 12: 'What we' (it is the same apostolic 'we', the plural of apostolic authority) 'have received is not the spirit of the world, but the Spirit who is from God' (namely the searching and knowing Spirit), 'so that we may understand what God has freely given us'. The apostles had, in fact, received two gracious gifts from God – the first, his grace in salvation ('what God has freely given us') and the second, his Spirit to enable them to understand his gracious salvation.

Paul himself is the best example of this double process. As we read his letters, he gives us a superb exposition of the gospel of God's grace. He tells us what God has done for guilty sinners like us who are without excuse and deserve nothing at his hand but judgment. He declares that God sent his Son to die for our sins on the cross and to rise again, and that if we are united to Jesus Christ, by faith inwardly and by baptism outwardly, then we die with him and rise again with him, and experience a new life in him. It is a magnificent gospel that Paul unfolds in his letters. But how does he know all this? How can he make such comprehensive statements of salvation? Well, the answer is, first, because he has himself received it. He knows the grace of God in experience. Then, second, the Holy Spirit has been given to him to interpret his own experience to him. Thus the Holy Spirit revealed to him God's plan of salvation, what Paul calls 'the mystery' in other epistles. The searching Spirit became the revealing Spirit.

The inspiring Spirit

Now we are ready for stage three: the revealing Spirit became the inspiring Spirit. Verse 13: 'This is what we speak, not in words taught us by human wisdom but in words taught by the Spirit.' Notice that in verse 12 Paul writes of what 'we have received', and in verse 13 of what 'we speak'. I might perhaps elaborate his sequence of thought like this: 'We have received these gracious gifts of God; we have received this Spirit to interpret to us what God has done for us and given to us; now, we impart to others what we have received.' The searching Spirit, who had revealed God's plan of salvation to the apostles, went on to communicate this gospel through the apostles to others. Just as the Spirit did not keep his researches to himself, so the apostles did not keep his revelation to themselves. No. They understood that they were trustees of it. They had to deliver to others what they had received.

Moreover, what they imparted was in words, and their words are specifically described as 'not taught us by human wisdom but in words taught us by the Spirit' (v. 13). Notice how the Holy Spirit is mentioned again, this time as the inspiring Spirit. For here in verse 13 is an unambiguous claim on the part of the apostle Paul to 'verbal inspiration'. That is to say, the very words with which the apostles clothed the message that had been revealed to them by the Spirit were words taught them by the same Spirit.

I strongly suspect that the reason why the idea of 'verbal inspiration' is unpopular today is that people misunderstand it. In consequence, what they are rejecting is not its true meaning, but a caricature. So let me try to clear the concept of some major misconceptions. First, 'verbal inspiration' does not mean that 'every word of the Bible is literally true'. No, we fully recognise that the biblical authors used many different literary genres, each of which must be interpreted according to its own rules – history as history, poetry as poetry, parable as parable, etc. What is inspired is the natural sense of the words, according to the author's intention, whether this is literal or figurative.

Second, 'verbal inspiration' does not mean verbal dictation. Muslims believe that Allah dictated the Quran to Muhammad, word by word, in Arabic. Christians do not believe this about the Bible for, as we have already seen and I shall further emphasise later, the Holy Spirit treated the biblical authors as persons, not machines. With a few minor exceptions they seem to have been in full possession of their faculties while the Spirit was communicating his Word through their words.

Third, 'verbal inspiration' does not mean that every sentence of the Bible is God's Word, even in isolation from its context. For not everything contained in the Bible is affirmed by the Bible. A good example is the long speeches of Job's so-called 'comforters'. Their major thesis repeated time and again – namely that God was punishing Job for his personal sins – was mistaken. In the last chapter God says to them twice, 'you have not spoken the truth about me' (42:7–8). So their words cannot be taken as God's words. They are included in order to be contradicted, not endorsed. The inspired Word of God is what is being affirmed, whether as instruction, command or promise.

'Verbal inspiration' means that what the Holy Spirit has spoken and still speaks through the human authors, understood according to the plain, natural meaning of the words used, is true and without error. There is no need at all to be embarrassed by this Christian belief, or to be ashamed or afraid of it. No, it is very reasonable, because words are the units of which sentences are made up. Words are the building blocks of speech. It is therefore impossible to frame a precise message without constructing precise sentences composed of precise words.

Let us imagine we could only use a few words, such as in a text message. We would want to send a message which will not only be understood, but which will not be misunderstood. So we would draft it carefully. We would delete a word here and we would add a word there, until we have polished our message to our satisfaction. Words matter. Every speaker who wants to communicate a message that will be understood and not misunderstood knows the importance of words. Every preacher who takes pains to prepare his sermons chooses his words with care. Every writer, whether of letters or articles or books, knows that words matter. Listen to what Charles Kingsley said in the middle of the nineteenth century: 'Without words we should know no more of each other's hearts and thoughts than the dog knows of his fellow dog for, if you will consider, you always think to yourself in words . . . without them all our thoughts would be mere blind longings, feelings which we could not understand ourselves.' So we have to clothe our thoughts in words.

This, then, is the apostolic claim, that the same Holy Spirit of God, who searches the depths of God and revealed his researches to the apostles, went on to communicate them through the apostles in words with which he himself supplied them. He spoke his words through their words, so that they were equally the words of God and the words of men. This is the double authorship of Scripture, which I have already mentioned. It is also the meaning of 'inspiration'. The inspiration of Scripture was not a mechanical process. It was intensely personal, for it involved a person (the Holy Spirit) speaking through persons (prophets and apostles) in such a way that, at the same time, his words were theirs, and their words were his.

The enlightening Spirit

We now come to the fourth stage in the Holy Spirit's work as the agent of revelation, and in this I shall describe him as the 'enlightening' Spirit. Let me set the scene.

How are we to think about the people who heard the apostles preaching and later read their letters? Were they left to fend for themselves? Were they obliged to struggle as best they could to understand the apostolic message? No. The same Spirit who was active in those who wrote the apostolic letters was also active in those who read them. So the Holy Spirit was working at both ends, as it were, inspiring the apostles and enlightening their hearers. This is already implied at the end of verse 13, a complicated phrase which has been interpreted in different ways. I take the Revised Standard Version translation as correct, namely that the Holy Spirit was 'interpreting spiritual truths to those

> The same Spirit who was active in those who wrote the apostolic letters was also active in those who read them

who possess the Spirit'. Possession of the Spirit was not limited to the biblical authors. Certainly his work of inspiration in them was unique, yet to this he added the Spirit's work of interpretation.

Verses 14 and 15 add to this truth, and are in stark contrast to each other. Verse 14 begins by referring to 'the person without the Spirit' (or 'the natural man', AV), that is, the unregenerate person who is not a Christian. Verse 15, however, begins with a reference to 'the person with the Spirit', the possessor of the Holy Spirit. So Paul divides mankind into two clear-cut categories: 'the natural' and 'the spiritual', that is, those who possess natural, animal or physical life, on the one hand, and on the other, those who have received spiritual or eternal life. The first category lacks the Holy Spirit because they have never been born again, but the Holy Spirit dwells in those to whom he has given a new birth. The indwelling of the Holy Spirit is, in fact, the distinguishing mark of the true Christian man and woman (Rom 8:9).

What difference does it make whether we have the Holy Spirit or not? All the difference in the world! Especially to our understanding of spiritual truth. The unspiritual or unregenerate person, who has not received the Holy Spirit, doesn't receive the things of the Spirit either, because they are foolishness to him (v. 14). Not only does he fail to understand them, he is not even able to do so because they are 'discerned only through the Spirit'. The spiritual person, on the other hand, the born-again Christian in whom the Holy Spirit dwells, 'discerns all things'. Not, of course, that he becomes omniscient like God, but that all those things to which he was previously blind, and which God has revealed in Holy Scripture, begin to make sense to him. He understands what he had never understood before, even though he himself is not really understood. Literally, he 'is not subject to merely human judgments'. He remains an enigma, for he has an inner secret of spiritual life and truth, which doesn't make sense to non-believers. This is hardly surprising, however, for nobody knows the mind of the Lord, or can instruct him. And since they cannot understand Christ's mind, they cannot understand ours either, though we whom the Holy Spirit enlightens can dare to say, 'we have the mind of Christ' (v. 16) – a truly amazing affirmation.

Is this your experience? Has the Bible become a new book to you? William Grimshaw, one of the great eighteenth-century evangelical leaders, told a friend after his conversion that 'if God had drawn up his Bible to heaven, and sent him down another, it could not have been newer to him'. It was a different book. I could say the same myself. I read the Bible daily before I was converted, because my mother brought me up to do so, but it was like a foreign language to me. I hadn't the slightest idea what it was all about. But when I was born again and the Holy Spirit came to dwell within me, the Bible immediately began to be a new book to me. Of course I am not claiming that I understood everything. I am far from understanding everything today. But I began to understand things I had never understood before. What a marvellous experience this is! Don't think of the Bible as just a collection of musty old documents whose real place is in a library. Don't think of the pages of Scripture as if they were fossils whose real place is behind glass in a museum. No, God speaks through what he has spoken. Through the ancient text of Scripture the Holy Spirit can communicate with us today freshly, personally and powerfully. 'Whoever has ears, let them hear what the Spirit says' (this is in the present tense, 'is saying') through the Scriptures to the churches (Rev 2:7, etc.).

> God speaks through what he has spoken

If the Holy Spirit speaks to us through the Scriptures today, you may be asking, why don't we all agree about everything? If the Spirit is the interpreter as well as the agent of God's revelation, why does he not lead us to a common mind? My answer to these questions may surprise you. It is that he does in fact enable us to agree much more than we disagree, and that we would agree with one another even more if we fulfilled the following four conditions.

First, *we must accept the supreme authority of Scripture*, and earnestly desire to submit to it. Among those who do so, there is already a lot of agreement. The big and painful differences which remain, for example between the Roman Catholic Church and the Protestant Churches, are mainly attributable to Rome's continuing unwillingness to declare that Scripture has supreme authority even over church traditions. Rome's official position (modified but not effectively altered by the Second Vatican Council) is still that 'both Sacred Tradition and Sacred Scripture are to be accepted and venerated with the same sense of devotion and reverence'. Now Protestants do not deny the importance of tradition, and some of us should have more respect for it, since the Holy Spirit has taught past generations of Christians and did not begin his instruction only with us! Nevertheless, when Scripture and tradition are in collision, we must allow Scripture to reform tradition, just as Jesus insisted with the 'traditions of the elders' (cf. Mark 7:1–13).

Second, *we must remember that the overriding purpose of Scripture is to bear witness to Christ* as the all-sufficient Saviour of sinners. When the sixteenth-century Reformers insisted on the clarity of Scripture, and translated the Bible so that ordinary people could read it for themselves, they were referring to the way of salvation. They did not deny that the Scriptures contain 'some things . . . hard to understand' (as Peter said of Paul's letters, 2 Pet 3:16); but they were eager to affirm that the essential truths of salvation were plain for all to understand.

Third, *we must apply sound principles of interpretation*. It is of course perfectly possible to twist the Bible into meaning anything we like. But our business is Scripture interpreting, not Scripture twisting. Above all, we have to seek both the original sense according to the biblical author's intention, and the natural sense, which may be either literal or figurative, again according to the author's intention. These are respectively the principles of history and of simplicity. When they are applied with integrity and rigour, then the Bible controls us rather than we who control the Bible. In consequence, the area of Christian agreement increases.

Fourth, *we must come to the biblical text with a recognition of our cultural prejudices* and with a willingness to have them challenged and changed. If we come to Scripture with the proud presupposition that all our inherited beliefs and practices are correct, then of course we shall find in the Bible only what we want to find, namely the comfortable confirmation of the status quo. As a result, we shall also find ourselves in sharp disagreement with people who come to Scripture from different backgrounds and with different convictions, and find these confirmed. There is probably no commoner source of discord than this. It is only when we are brave and humble enough to allow the Spirit of God through the Word of God radically to call in question our most cherished opinions, that we are likely to find fresh unity through fresh understanding.

The 'spiritual discernment' which the Holy Spirit promises is not given in defiance of these four commonplace conditions; it assumes that they are accepted and fulfilled.

Conclusion

We have considered the Holy Spirit in four roles, as the searching Spirit, the revealing Spirit, the inspiring Spirit and the enlightening Spirit. These are the four stages of his teaching ministry:

- First, he searches the depths of God and knows the thoughts of God.
- Second, he revealed his researches to the apostles.
- Third, he communicated through the apostles what he had revealed to them, and did so in words that he himself supplied.
- Fourth, he enlightened the minds of the hearers, so that they could discern what he had revealed to and through the apostles, and he continues this work of illumination today in those who are willing to receive it.

Two very simple and short lessons as we finish. The first is about *our view of the Holy Spirit*. There is much discussion today about the person and work of the Spirit, and this is only one of many passages in the Bible about him. But let me ask you this: is there room in your doctrine of the Spirit for this passage? Jesus called him 'the Spirit of truth'. So truth is very important to the Holy Spirit. Oh, I know, he is also the Spirit of holiness, and the Spirit of love, and the Spirit of power, but is he to you the Spirit of truth? According to the verses we have been studying, he is deeply concerned about the truth. He searches it, has revealed and communicated it, and enlightens our minds to grasp it. Dear friend, never denigrate truth! Never disdain theology! Never despise your mind! If you do, you grieve the Holy Spirit of truth. This passage should affect our view of the Holy Spirit.

Second, *our need of the Holy Spirit*. Do you want to grow in your knowledge of God? Of course you do. Do you want to grow in your understanding of the wisdom of God and of the totality of his purpose to make us one day like Christ in glory? Of course you do. So do I. Then we need the Holy Spirit, the Spirit of truth, to illumine our minds. For that we need to be born again. I sometimes wonder if the reason why some secular theologians today are speaking and writing, if I may say so,

> We need the Holy Spirit, the Spirit of truth, to illumine our minds

such rubbish (I am referring, for example, to their denial of a personality to God and of deity to Jesus) is that they have never been born again. It is possible to be a theologian and unregenerate. Is that why they do not discern these marvellous truths of Scripture? Scripture is spiritually discerned. So we need to come to the Scriptures humbly, reverently and expectantly. We need to acknowledge that the truths revealed in the Bible are still locked and sealed until the Holy Spirit opens them to us and opens our minds to them. For God hides them from the wise and clever, and reveals them only to 'babies', those who are humble and reverent in their approach to him. So then, before we preachers prepare, before a congregation listens, before an individual or a group begins to read the Bible – in these situations we must pray for the Holy Spirit's illumination: 'Open my eyes that I may see wonderful things in your law' (Ps 119:18). And he will.

4

The Church and the Bible

So far we have engaged in a Trinitarian study. We have seen that *God* is the author, *Christ* both the principal subject and the authenticating witness, and the *Holy Spirit* the agent of the great process of revelation. We come now to the church.

What do you think of the church? Your answer will probably depend on whether you are thinking about the ideal or the reality. In the ideal, the church is the most marvellous new creation of God. It is the new community of Jesus, enjoying a multi-racial, multi-national and multi-cultural harmony, which is unique in history and in contemporary society. The church is even the 'new humanity', the forerunner of a redeemed and renewed human race. It is a people who spend their earthly lives (as they will also spend eternity) in the loving service of God and of others. What a noble and beautiful ideal! In reality, however, the church is us (if you will pardon the bad grammar) – a crowd of sinful, fallible, squabbling, foolish, shallow Christians, who constantly fall short of God's ideal, and often fail even to approximate to it.

Now, what is the reason for this gap between the ideal and the reality? Why is the church in such a terrible condition throughout the world today – weak, broken up, and making so little impact upon the world for Christ? I'm sure there are many reasons, but I believe the overwhelming reason is what Amos called 'a famine . . . of hearing the words of the Lord' (Amos 8:11), or in plain modern language, a neglect of the Bible. The multiple unfaithfulness of the church is due to its overriding unfaithfulness to the self-revelation of God in Scripture. Dr Martyn Lloyd-Jones was right when he wrote in his book, 'Preaching and Preachers', that 'the decadent eras and periods of the church's history have always been those in which preaching has declined'. In other words, the church remains sick and feeble whenever it refuses the healing medicine and wholesome nourishment of the Word of God.

We are now going to consider two texts, both of which use an architectural metaphor.

In Ephesians 2:20 the church, which has just been defined as God's 'household' or family (v. 19), is also described as 'built on the foundation of the apostles and prophets, with Christ Jesus himself as the chief cornerstone'. That is, the teaching of the biblical authors is the foundation on which the church is built, as Jesus Christ is the cornerstone which holds it together.

In 1 Timothy 3:15 the metaphor is reversed. Having again called the church 'God's household', Paul now goes on to call it 'the pillar and foundation of the truth'.

You see in the first passage the *truth* is the foundation, and the *church* is the building it supports, while in the second text, the *church* is the foundation, and the *truth* is the building which it supports.

'Well, there you are', I think I hear somebody saying. 'I told you so. The Bible is full of contradictions.' Really? Wait a moment. Both these verses come from the pen of the same man, the apostle Paul. Let us give him credit for a little logical consistency. We have to ask at what point the analogy is being made, in order to understand what the author is intending to say through the figure of speech that he is using. When we apply this principle to our two texts, we find (as we would expect) that they are beautifully complementary.

You ask how, at the same time, the truth can be the foundation of the church and the church the foundation of the truth? Well, let me suggest the answer. What Paul is affirming in Ephesians 2:20 is that the church depends upon the truth for its existence. It rests upon the teaching of the apostles and prophets, and without their teaching (now recorded in Scripture) the church could neither exist nor survive, let alone flourish. But according to 1 Timothy 3:15 the truth depends on the church for its defence and propagation. The church is called to serve the truth by holding it firm against attack, and by holding it high before the eyes of the world. Thus, *the church needs the Bible* because it is built on it. And *the church serves the Bible* by holding it fast and making it known. These are the two complementary truths that we are going to investigate further.

The church needs the Bible

There are many ways in which the church depends on the Bible. Let me give you a few examples.

a) The Bible created the church

This statement could be misleading when put this starkly. It could even be dismissed as inaccurate. For it is true that the Old Testament church as the people of God existed for centuries before the Bible was complete. And the New Testament church also existed for a long time before the New Testament canon was finalised, and longer still before the first Bible was printed for publication. Moreover, you may rightly say, the first-century church 'shaped' the New Testament, in the sense that the Christian community shared in determining in what form the words and works of Jesus would be recorded. The church was thus the place within which the Bible came to be written and treasured. I agree with all these qualifications. Nevertheless, I repeat, the Bible may be said to have created the church. Or, more accurately, the Word of God (which is now written in the Bible) created the church. For how did the Christian church come into being? Answer: by the preaching of the apostles, who spoke not in the name of the church, but in the name of Christ.

At Pentecost the prophetic witness of the Old Testament was added to by Peter's testimony as apostle. He proclaimed Jesus as Messiah and Lord, the Holy Spirit confirmed his words with power, and the believing people of God became the Spirit-filled Body of Christ. God himself performed this creative work by his Spirit through his Word. Moreover he continued to honour the preaching of the apostles in the same way. On his famous missionary journeys Paul also bore witness to Christ, arguing that the testimony of the apostolic eyewitnesses was in full harmony with the Old Testament Scriptures. Many listened, repented, believed and were baptised, so that churches were planted all over the Roman Empire. How? By the Word of God. God's Word (the combined witness of prophets and apostles), proclaimed in the power of the Spirit, created the church. It still does. The church is built on that foundation. And when the canon of the New Testament came to be determined, the church did not give authority to these documents, but simply *acknowledged* the authority they already possessed. Why? Because they were 'apostolic' and contained the teaching of the Lord's apostles.

For these reasons, we may truthfully say that the Bible (that is, the Word of God now written in the Bible) created and creates the church.

b) The Bible sustains the church

The Creator always sustains what he has created, and since he has brought the church into being, he keeps it in being. Moreover, having created it by his Word, he sustains and nourishes it by his Word. If it is true, as Jesus said, quoting Deuteronomy (Matt 4:4; cf. Deut 8:3), that human beings live 'not on bread alone, but on every word that comes from the mouth of God', it is also true of churches. They cannot flourish without it. The church needs constantly to hear God's Word. For this reason preaching is central in public worship. Preaching is not an intrusion into it but rather indispensable to it. For the worship of God is always a response to the Word of God. That is why, for example it is good in the worship services of the church if there is an movement back and forth between Word and worship. First God speaks his Word (in Scripture sentence, readings and exposition), and then the people respond in confession, creed, praise and prayer. The Christian congregation grows into maturity in Jesus Christ only as they hear, receive, believe, absorb and obey the Word of God.

> Preaching is not an intrusion into it but rather indispensable to it. For the worship of God is always a response to the Word of God

c) The Bible directs the church

Christians are pilgrims on their way to an eternal home. They are travelling through land that is barren, pathless, hostile and dark. They need guidance for the way, and God has provided it. 'Your word is a lamp for my feet and a light on my path' (Ps 119:105). I agree, of course, that what is called the 'hermeneutical' task (the task of interpreting the Scriptures) is difficult. Scripture does not give us slick answers to complex twenty-first-century problems. We have to wrestle with the text, with both its meaning and its application, and do so in prayer, study and fellowship with each other. Nevertheless, the principles we need to guide us are there in the Bible and together we can discover, through the illumination of the Holy Spirit, how to apply them to our lives in the world today.

d) The Bible reforms the church

In every century, I am sorry to say, including our own, the church has deviated to some degree from God's truth and from his ethical standards. As the former missionary statesman, Max Warren, wrote, church history is 'a bitter sweet story' in which the most outstanding fact is the infinite patience of God with his people. If then the church is constantly deviant, how can it be reformed? Answer: only by the Word of God. The greatest church renewal there has ever been in the history of the world was the sixteenth-century Reformation, and it was due, more than anything else, to a recovery of the Bible.

e) The Bible unites the church

Every Christian conscience should be troubled by the disunity of the church. I hope we have not grown used to it. The visible unity of the church is surely a proper goal of Christian endeavour (although we may not all agree with one another what precise form it should take). So what is the basic reason for our continuing disunity? It is the lack of an agreed *authority*. So long as churches follow their own traditions and speculations, the universal church will continue to splinter. Once churches confess the supreme authority of Scripture, however, and its sole sufficiency for salvation, and are determined to judge their traditions by its teaching, then at once the way is opened for them to find unity in truth. The Bible unites the church when the church submits to it.

f) The Bible revives the church

We long for revival, for that special, unusual, supernatural visitation by God, which makes the whole community aware of his living and holy presence. Sinners are convicted, repenters converted, backsliders restored, enemies reconciled, believers transformed, and dead churches brought back to life. But how does revival happen? Only by a sovereign work of the Holy Spirit of God. But what means does the Holy Spirit use? He uses his Word. The Word of God is 'the sword of the Spirit' (Eph 6:17; cf. Heb 4:12) which he wields in his work in the world. Never separate the Spirit of God from the Word of God, for when the Holy Spirit uses this weapon in his sovereign power, he pricks the conscience, cuts out cancerous growths from the body of Christ and puts the devil to flight. It is the Bible that revives the church.

> Sinners are convicted, repenters converted, backsliders restored, enemies reconciled, believers transformed, and dead churches brought back to life

Are you convinced? I hope so. *The church needs the Bible.* The church depends on the Bible. The church is built upon the foundation of the apostles and prophets. The Bible is indispensable to the church's life, growth, nurture, direction, reformation, unity and renewal. The church cannot exist without the Bible.

This leads to the second and complementary truth: if the church needs the Bible, the Bible also needs the church. If the church depends on the Bible, the Bible also depends on the church. For the church is called to serve the Bible by guarding and spreading its message.

> The Bible is indispensable to the church's life, growth, nurture, direction, reformation, unity and renewal. The church cannot exist without the Bible

The church serves the Bible

Although God spoke his Word through prophets and apostles, it had to be received and written down. Today it still needs to be translated, printed, published, distributed, preached, defended, broadcast, televised and dramatised. In these and other ways the church is serving the Bible, guarding it and making it known.

This explains why Paul wrote in 1 Timothy 3:15 that the church is 'the pillar and foundation of the truth'. The two words he used are instructive. The church is both the foundation (or buttress) of the truth on the one hand, and the pillar of the truth on the other. Foundations and buttresses hold a building firm; pillars hold it high, thrusting it aloft for people to see. This suggests both the apologetic task and the evangelistic task of the church. For, as the foundation or buttress of the truth, the church must hold it firm and defend it against heretics, so that the truth remains steadfast and immovable. But, as the pillar of the truth, the church must hold it high, making it visible to the world, so that people may see it and believe. So the Bible needs the church to *protect* it and to *spread* it.

There is an urgent need for both these responsibilities. On the one hand, heresy is gaining ground in the church. There are false teachers who deny the infinite, loving personality of Almighty God, and others who deny the deity of our Lord Jesus Christ, as well as the authority of the Bible. These heretics seem to be increasing, and are spreading their dangerous ideas by books and sermons, on radio and television. So the truth needs buttresses – Christian scholars who will give their lives to what Paul called 'defending and confirming the gospel' (Phil 1:7). Is God calling some younger theologian who is reading these words to be a buttress of the truth in the church, to hold it firm, to defend it against heresy and misunderstanding? What a vocation! The church must guard and demonstrate the truth.

At the same time, the church is called to preach the gospel throughout the world. There are millions of people in the world who have never really heard of Jesus, and there are many more who, having heard of him, have never believed in him. 'How can they hear without someone preaching to them?' (Rom 10:14). The church needs pioneer evangelists who will develop new forms of mission in order to penetrate closed areas, especially the Islamic and the secular worlds. For the church is the pillar of the truth. So we have got to hold it high and make it known, so that people may see it in its beauty and adequacy, and embrace it for themselves.

Conclusion

The church needs the Bible and the Bible needs the church. Those are the complementary truths which Paul's two statements express. The church could not survive without the Bible to sustain it, and the Bible could hardly survive without the church to guard and spread it. Each needs the other. The Bible and the church are inseparable twins. Once we have got hold of that, three exhortations follow.

First, I exhort *Christian pastors* to take preaching more seriously. Our calling is to study and expound the Word of God, and relate it to the modern world. The health of every congregation depends more than anything else on the quality of its preaching ministry. This may surprise you. I know, of course, that church members can grow into maturity in Christ in spite of their pastors,

> The health of every congregation depends more than anything else on the quality of its preaching ministry

and even when their pastors are bad and neglectful. For they can pray and read the Scriptures both by themselves and in fellowship groups, and today good resources are available as a valuable supplementary means of instruction. Nevertheless, the New Testament indicates that God's purpose is to commit the care of his people to pastors, who are so to proclaim Christ to them out of the Scriptures, in the glory of his person and work, that their worship, faith and obedience are drawn out from them. That is why I dare to say that, more often than not, the pew is a reflection of the pulpit, and that the pew does not normally rise higher than the pulpit. So then, my fellow pastors, let us determine afresh to give ourselves to this priority task!

Second, I exhort *Christian people*, not only to study the Bible yourselves in your home and in your fellowship group, but also to demand (it is not too strong a word) faithful, biblical preaching from your pastors. Let me put it like this: the ministry you get is the ministry you deserve, and the ministry you deserve is the ministry you demand! Lay people have much more power in the churches than they commonly realise. They join a church where the Bible is hardly ever preached, and they passively accept it and do nothing about it! There may be times when you need to have the courage to reprove your pastors because you perceive that they are not being diligent in their study and faithful in their exposition. But don't give us only your reproof; give us your encouragement and your prayers. Set your pastors free from the distracting burden of administration. Pastoral oversight should also be shared by the lay leaders of the congregation. Every generation needs to re-learn the lesson of Acts 6, where the apostles refused to be deflected from the teaching role to which Christ had called them. They delegated certain social and administrative tasks, in order to devote themselves 'to prayer and the ministry of the word' (Acts 6:1–4). It is the lay leaders of the congregation who can ensure that the same priority is recognised today.

Third, I want to exhort *Christian parents*. Teach the Bible to your children. Don't surrender this parental responsibility to the church, even, or to the school; do it yourselves, so that your children, like Timothy, come to know the Holy Scriptures from childhood (2 Tim 3:15). If you do this, then the next generation of church leaders which arises will grasp, as the present generation doesn't always seem to, the indispensable place of the Bible in the church.

So let us enthrone the Bible in the home and in the church, not because we worship it but because God speaks through it. Then, as we hear his voice again, the church will be renewed, reformed and revived, and will become what God has always intended it to be – a bright light shining in the darkness around us.

5

The Christian and the Bible

L et me rehearse briefly the ground we have covered. We have thought about:

- 'God and the Bible' because he is its author;
- 'Christ and the Bible' because he is its subject;
- 'The Holy Spirit and the Bible' because he was the means of its inspiration;
- 'The Church and the Bible' because the church is built upon it and is called to guard its treasures and make them known.

We conclude with something more personal and individual – 'the Christian and the Bible'.

I do not hesitate to say that the Bible is indispensable to every Christian's health and growth. Christians who neglect the Bible simply do not mature. When Jesus quoted from Deuteronomy that human beings do not live by bread only but by God's Word, he was saying that the Word of God is just as necessary for spiritual health as food is for bodily health. I am not now thinking of Christians into whose language the Bible has not yet been translated, or of illiterate people who may have the Bible in their language but are unable to read it for themselves. To be sure, such people are not altogether cut off from the nourishment of God's Word, for they can still receive it from a pastor, missionary, relative or friend. I am bound to say, however, that I think their

> The Word of God is just as necessary for spiritual health as food is for bodily health

Christian life would be enriched if they could have direct access to the Scriptures, which is why such heroic work has been done to have the Bible translated into the languages of the world. I am not thinking of these situations. I am thinking rather about Christians who have the Bible in their own language. Our problem is not that the Bible is unavailable to us, but that we do not take advantage of its availability. We need to read and meditate on it daily, to study it in a fellowship group and to hear it expounded during Sunday worship. Otherwise we shall not grow. Growth into maturity in Christ depends upon a close acquaintance with, and a believing response to, the Bible.

I want to try to answer the question which may be forming in your minds: just how and why does the Bible enable us to grow? As an illustration of its effectiveness as a means of grace I have chosen the story of Jesus' washing of his disciple's feet, recorded in John 13. When he had finished, put on his outer garment again and returned to his place, he immediately referred to himself as their teacher: 'You call me "Teacher" and "Lord", and rightly so, for that is what I am' (v. 13). The implication is clear, that through his act of foot-washing he had been teaching them certain truths and lessons which he wanted them to learn. There seem to have been three.

a) He was teaching them about himself

Jesus' actions were a deliberate parable of his mission. John seems clearly to have understood this, for he introduces the incident with these words: 'Jesus knew . . . that he had come from God and was returning to God; so he got up from the meal . . . ' (vv. 3–4). That is, knowing these things, he dramatised them in action. Perhaps the best commentary is Philippians 2, which unfolds the stages of his self-humbling before he was highly exalted. Thus Jesus 'got up from the meal', as he had risen from his heavenly throne. He 'took off his outer clothing', as he had laid aside his glory and emptied himself of it. He then 'wrapped a towel round his waist' (the badge of servitude), as in the incarnation he had taken the form of a servant. Next, he began 'to wash his disciples' feet, drying them with the towel', as he went to the cross to secure our cleansing from sin. After this he put back on 'his clothes, and returned to his place', as he returned to his heavenly glory and sat down at the Father's right hand. By these actions, he was dramatising his whole earthly career. He was teaching them about himself, who he was, where he had come from and where he was going.

b) He was teaching them about his salvation

He said to Peter, 'Unless I wash you, you have no part with me' (v. 8). In other words, the forgiveness of sin is necessary in order to enjoy fellowship with Jesus Christ. Until and unless we have been washed, we cannot have anything to do with him. More subtly still, Jesus distinguished between two different kinds of washing: the bath, on the one hand, and the washing of feet, on the other. The apostles were familiar with this social distinction. Before visiting a friend's home they would take a bath. Then on arrival at their friend's a servant would wash their feet. They wouldn't need another bath, but only a foot-washing. Jesus seems to have used this well-known cultural distinction to teach a less well-known theological distinction: when we first come to him in penitence and faith we get a bath and are washed all over. Theologically, it is called 'justification' or 'regeneration', and is symbolised in baptism. Then, when we fall into sin as Christians, what we need is not another bath (we cannot be re-justified or re-baptised) but a foot-washing; that is, the cleansing of a daily forgiveness. So Jesus says in verse 10: 'those who have had a bath need only to wash their feet; their whole body is clean.'

c) He was teaching them about his will

Before sitting down for the meal in the upper room, the apostles had been squabbling about who was to have the best seats. They were so preoccupied with questions of precedence that they sat down to the meal unwashed. Evidently there had been no servant to wash their feet, and it hadn't occurred to them that one of them might assume that lowly role and wash the feet of the others. So during supper Jesus did what none of them would have demeaned himself to do. Next, when he had finished, he said to them, 'Now that I, your Lord and Teacher, have washed your feet, you also should wash one another's feet. I have set you an example that you should do as I have done for you. Very truly I tell you, no servant is greater than his master . . .

Now that you know these things, you will be blessed if you do them' (vv. 14–17). Our Lord stooped to serve. It is his will that we do so too.

Here, then, were Jesus' three lessons from one incident – first about his *person* (that he had come from God and was going to God), second about his *salvation* (that after the bath of justification we need only the continuous washing of our feet) and third about his *will* (that we must wash one another's feet, that is, express our love for one another in humble service). Or put another way, he taught three lessons which required three responses. In giving them a revelation of himself, he was asking for their *worship*. In giving them a promise of salvation, he was asking for their *trust*. In giving them a commandment to love and serve one another, he was asking for their *obedience*.

> Our Lord stooped to serve. It is his will that we do so too

I do not think it an exaggeration to claim that all the teaching of the Bible can be divided into these three categories, requiring these three responses. For throughout Scripture there are:

- revelations of God demanding our worship,
- promises of salvation demanding our faith,
- commandments about our duty demanding our obedience.

Having considered the foot-washing as one example, let us look at this threefold pattern a little more fully.

Revelations of God

The Bible is God's self-disclosure, the divine autobiography. In the Bible, God is speaking about God. He makes himself known progressively in the rich variety of his being: as the *Creator* of the universe and of human beings in his own image, the climax of his creation; as the *living God* who sustains and animates everything he has made; as the *covenant God* who chose Abraham, Isaac, Jacob and their descendants to be his special people; and as a *gracious God* who is slow to anger and quick to forgive, but also as a *righteous God* who punishes idolatry and injustice among his own people as well as in the pagan nations. Then in the New Testament he reveals himself as the *Father of our Lord and Saviour Jesus Christ*, who sent him into the world to take our nature upon him, to be born and grow, live and teach, work and suffer, die and rise, occupy the throne and send the Holy Spirit; next as *the God of the new covenant community*, the church, who sends his people into the world as his witnesses and his servants in the power of the Holy Spirit; and finally as *the God who one day will send Jesus Christ in power and glory* – to save, to judge and to reign, who will create a new universe, and who in the end will be everything to everybody.

This majestic revelation of God (Father, Son and Holy Spirit), which unfolds from the creation to the consummation, moves us to worship. When we catch these glimpses of the greatness of God, of his glory and grace, we fall down on our faces before him and bring to him the homage of our lips, our hearts and our lives. It is impossible to read the Bible with any sensitivity and not be a worshipper. The Word of God evokes the worship of God.

> It is impossible to read the Bible with any sensitivity and not be a worshipper. The Word of God evokes the worship of God

Promises of salvation

We have already seen that God's main purpose in giving us the Bible is to 'make you wise for salvation through faith in Christ Jesus' (2 Tim 3:15). So the Bible tells the story of Jesus, pointing to him in the Old Testament, describing his earthly career in the Gospels, and unfolding in the epistles the fullness of his person and work. More than that, the Scripture does not just present Jesus to us as our all-sufficient Saviour; it urges us to go to him and put our trust in him. And it promises us that, if we do so, we shall receive the forgiveness of our sins and the gift of the liberating Holy Spirit. The Bible is full of salvation promises. It promises new life in the new community to those who respond to the call of Jesus Christ. Jesus gave one such promise to Peter in the incident of the foot-washing when he said to him, 'You are clean' (John 13:10). Peter's mind must often have grasped that promise and believed it. Even after he had denied Jesus, he was not rejected. Of course he needed to repent, to be forgiven, to be re-commissioned. But he did not need another bath, since already he had been made clean. The words of Jesus must have reassured his heart and given peace to his nagging conscience.

In the seventeenth century, an English preacher called John Bunyan wrote an allegory about the Christian life, called 'Pilgrim's Progress', in which he described the challenges of two travellers, Christian and Hopeful. At one point in the story, they found themselves in the grounds of Doubting Castle, owned by Giant Despair. They were captured by the Giant and feared for their lives: there seemed no possibility of escape. Then, on the third day, at about midnight, 'they began to pray, and continued in prayer till almost break of day'. A little before then, Christian had realised that he had a key called Promise 'that will, I am persuaded, open any lock in Doubting Castle'. With Hopeful's encouragement, Christian tried the key, and 'it flew open with ease.' With the key they were able to escape through the dungeon door, the outer door, and the iron gate of the castle, and the Giant was unable to stop them.

You too have a key called Promise, for God has given it to you in the Scriptures. Have you ever used it to escape from Doubting Castle? When Satan harasses our conscience, and tries to persuade us that there is no forgiveness for such sinners as we are, only a trustful reliance on God's promises to the penitent can liberate us from his harassment. When we're confused, we have to learn to rest on the promise of his guidance; when we're afraid, on the promise of his protection; when we're lonely, on the promise of his presence. The promises of God can guard our hearts and minds, his promises of salvation.

> When we're confused, we have to learn to rest on the promise of his guidance; when we're afraid, on the promise of his protection; when we're lonely, on the promise of his presence

Here we should mention baptism and the Lord's Supper. They are visible signs to which promises are attached. It is obvious that the water of baptism and the bread and wine of Communion are outward and visible signs. More particularly, however, they are signs of God's grace, signs which visibly promise his cleansing, forgiveness and new life to those who repent and believe in Jesus. So they encourage and strengthen our faith.

Commandments to obey

In calling out a people for himself, God told them what kind of people he wanted them to be. They were a special people; he expected from them special conduct. So he gave them the Ten Commandments as a summary of his will, which Jesus underlined in his Sermon on the Mount, uncovering their disturbing implications. The righteousness of his disciples, he said, must 'surpass' the righteousness of the scribes and Pharisees (Matt 5:20). It would be 'greater' in the sense that it would be deeper, a righteousness of the heart, a glad and radical inward obedience.

It is particularly important in our day to emphasise God's call to moral obedience, because at least two groups of people are denying it. First, there are those who argue that God's one and only absolute command is love, that all other laws have been effectively abolished, and that love is by itself a sufficient guide to Christian conduct. Whatever is expressive of love is good, they say; whatever is incompatible with it is evil. Now certainly true love (the sacrifice of self in the service of others) is the pre-eminent Christian virtue, and to follow its dictates is extremely demanding. Nevertheless, love needs guidelines, and it is this direction that God's commandments supply. Love does not dispense with law; it fulfils it (Rom 13:8–10).

Second, there are evangelical Christians who interpret Paul's assertions that 'Christ is the culmination of the law' (Rom 10:4) and that 'you are not under law but under grace' (Rom 6:14) as meaning that Christians are no longer under obligation to obey God's moral law. To try to do so, they say, is a 'legalism' which contradicts the freedom Christ has given us. But they misunderstand Paul. The 'legalism' Paul rejected was not obedience to God's law in itself, but the attempt by such obedience to win God's favour and forgiveness. This is impossible, he wrote, for 'no one will be declared righteous in God's sight by the works of the law' (Rom 3:20).

However, once justified by God's sheer grace (that is, declared righteous in his sight by his free and undeserved favour through Christ), we are then under obligation to keep his law, and *want* to do so. Indeed, Christ died for us precisely 'in order that the righteous requirement of the law might be fully met in us' (Rom 8:3–4), and God puts his Spirit in our hearts in order to write his law there (Jer 31:33; Ezek 36:27; Gal 5:22–23). Our Christian freedom, therefore, is freedom to obey, not to disobey. As Jesus said several times, if we love him we shall keep his commandments (John 14:15, 21–24, 15:14). And it is in Scripture that God's commandments are to be found.

So in the Bible God gives us:

- revelations of himself which lead us to worship,
- promises of salvation which stimulate our faith,
- commandments expressing his will which demand our obedience.

This is the meaning of Christian discipleship. Its three essential ingredients are worship, faith and obedience. And all three are inspired by the Word of God. *Worship* is the response to God's self-revelation. It is an adoring preoccupation with the glory of God. *Faith* is a restful confidence in the promises of God. It delivers us from the fluctuations of religious experience - up and down, up and down, Sunday night, Monday morning. Nothing can deliver you from that but the promises of God, for our feelings fluctuate, but

> Our Christian freedom, therefore, is freedom to obey, not to disobey

God's Word remains forever firm. *Obedience* is a loving commitment to the will of God. It rescues us from the bog of moral relativism and sets our feet upon the rock of God's absolute commands.

Moreover, worship, faith and obedience – the three ingredients of discipleship – are all outward looking. In worship we are preoccupied with God's glory, in faith with his promises, in obedience with his commands. Authentic Christian discipleship is never introverted. The Bible is a marvellously liberating book. It pulls us out of ourselves, and makes us instead obsessed with God, his glory, promises and will. To love God like this (and to love others for his sake) is to be set free from the awful chains of our own self-centredness. The Christian who is engrossed in himself becomes paralysed, and only God's Word can deliver us from the paralysis which comes from such self-preoccupation.

Conclusion

The vital place of the Bible in the Christian life exposes the seriousness of liberal theology. By undermining public confidence in the reliability of the Bible, it makes Christian discipleship all but impossible. Let me explain. All Christians agree that discipleship includes worship, faith and obedience. Worship, faith and obedience are essential parts of our Christian life. We cannot live as Christians without them. Yet none is possible without a reliable Bible.

How can we worship God if we don't know who he is, what he is like or what kind of worship is pleasing to him? Christians are not Athenians who worship an unknown God. We must know God before we can worship him. And it is the Bible which tells us what he is like.

Again, how can we believe or trust in God if we don't know his promises? Faith is not a synonym for superstition, or for believing without evidence. Faith is a reasoning trust. It rests on the promises of God, and on the character of the God who made them. Without promises our faith shrivels up and dies. And God's promises are found in the Bible.

Again, how can we obey God, if we don't know his will and commandments? Christian obedience is not blind obedience, but open-eyed and loving. For God has given us commandments in the Bible, and shown us that they are not burdensome.

So then, without God's revelation worship is impossible; without God's promises faith is impossible; without God's commandments obedience is impossible. Therefore without the Bible discipleship is impossible.

Do we realise how blessed we are to have a Bible in our hands? God has graciously made provision for our discipleship. He has revealed to us himself, his salvation and his will. He has made it possible for us to worship him, trust him and obey

> Without God's revelation worship is impossible; without God's promises faith is impossible; without God's commandments obedience is impossible. Therefore without the Bible discipleship is impossible

him, in other words, to live as his loving children in the world. We need then to come expectantly to the Bible each day. The great curse of our Bible reading, whenever it becomes just a stale and boring routine, is that we do not come to it expectantly. We don't come with confidence that God is willing, able and anxious to speak to us through his Word. We need to come to the Bible every day with the petition of Samuel on our lips, 'Master, speak, your servant is listening.' And he will! Sometimes through his Word he will give us a revelation of himself; we shall perceive something of his glory; our heart will be deeply moved within us; and we shall fall down and worship him. Sometimes through his Word he will give us a promise; we shall grasp it, lay hold of it, and say, 'Lord, I'm not going to let it go until I inherit it, and until it becomes true of me.' Sometimes through the Bible he will give us a command; we shall see our need to repent of our disobedience; and we shall pray and resolve that by his grace we shall obey it in years to come.

> We need to come to the Bible every day with the petition of Samuel on our lips, 'Master, speak, your servant is listening.' And he will!

These revelations, promises and commandments we will store up in our mind until our Christian memory becomes like a well-stocked cupboard. Then in moments of need we shall be able to take down from its shelves truths or promises or commandments which are appropriate to the situation in which we find ourselves. Without this, we condemn ourselves to never becoming mature. Only if we meditate on God's Word, listen to God speaking to us, hear his voice, and respond to him in worship, faith and obedience, will we grow into maturity in Christ.

Postscript

I have been concerned in this little book both about the Bible's 'yesterday' (where it came from) and about its 'today' (what it means for us). I have tried to develop a simple, Trinitarian doctrine of Scripture as a message which:

- comes from God (he spoke it and speaks it),
- focuses on Christ (he witnesses to it as witnessing to him),
- and was articulated by the Holy Spirit through the human authors (so that his words and theirs coincided).

The practical usefulness of the Bible today, both for the church and for the individual Christian, depends on our acceptance of its divine origin and purpose. Paul himself combined these things when he described all Scripture as being on the one hand 'God-breathed' and on the other 'useful' (2 Tim 3:16–17). It is useful for us 'for teaching, rebuking, correcting and training in righteousness', precisely because it was breathed out of the mouth of God. So our view of the Bible and our use of it go together. It matters what we think about it.

I am deeply disturbed by the casual attitude to the Bible adopted by many, and so I long to see it reinstated in the hearts and homes of Christian people, and enthroned in the pulpits of the world. Only then can the church again hear and heed God's Word. Only then will God's people learn to tie together their faith and their life, as they seek to apply the teaching of Scripture to their moral standards, economic lifestyle, marriage and family, work and citizenship. Only then can Christians hope to be the world's salt

> I long to see it reinstated in the hearts and homes of Christian people, and enthroned in the pulpits of the world. Only then can the church again hear and heed God's Word

and light, as Jesus said they were to be, and influence their country's culture, its institutions and laws, its values and ideals.

The practical profitability of Scripture – for church and Christian, home and nation – should not, however, be our main reason for desiring its reinstatement, but rather the glory of God. If the Bible may rightly be called 'the Word of God' (though spoken through the words of men), then clearly to neglect it is to neglect *him*, while to listen to it is to listen to him. The overriding reason why we should 'let the message of Christ dwell among you richly' (Col 3:16) is not that we shall thereby be enriched, but that he will thereby be honoured and glorified. He wants us to have a Christian mind as well as to live a Christian life. But to have a Christian mind we must have *his* mind, 'the mind of Christ' (cf. 1 Cor 2:16; Phil 2:5). And our mind can be conformed to his mind only as it becomes soaked in his Word. That is why we need *God's Word for today's world*.

> Our mind can be conformed to his mind only as it becomes soaked in his Word

Further Reading

Revelation, inspiration and authority

God Has Spoken by J. I. Packer (Baker, 978-0-80107-128-7, 3rd ed. 1994).

Know the Truth by Bruce Milne (IVP UK, 978-1-78359-103-9, 3rd ed. 2014), Part I.

Taking God at His Word by Kevin DeYoung (IVP UK, 978-1-78359-122-0, 2014)

Words of Life by Timothy Ward (IVP UK, 978-1-84474-207-3, 2009)

Understanding the Bible

Understanding the Bible by John R. W. Stott (Scripture Union, 978-1-85999-640-9, Rev ed. 2003).

Knowing Scripture by R. C. Sproul (IVP US, 978-083083-723-6, 2nd ed. 2009), chapters 3-5.

A Guide to Interpreting Scripture by Michael Kyomya (Hippobooks, 978-9-96600-308-9, 2010)

Introducing the Old Testament by John Drane (Lion Hudson, 978-0-74595-503-2, 2010)

Introducing the New Testament by John Drane (Lion Hudson, 978-0-74595-504-9, 2010)

Studying the Bible

Knowing Scripture by R. C. Sproul (IVP US, 978-083083-723-6, 2nd ed. 2009), chapters 1-2 and 6.

Dig Deeper by Andrew Sach (IVP UK, 978-184474-431-2, 2010)

Dig Even Deeper by Andrew Sach (IVP UK, 978-184474-432-9, 2011)

The Unity of the Bible

God's Big Picture by Vaughan Roberts (IVP UK, 978-184474-370-4, 2009)

Biblical Theology in the Life of the Church by Michael Lawrence (Crossway, 978-143351-508-8, 2010)

From Creation to New Creation by Tim Chester (Good Book, 978-190831-785-8, 2010)

Salvation Belongs to Our God by Christopher J. H. Wright (Langham Global Library, 9781907713071, 2013)

Langham Literature and its imprints are a ministry of Langham Partnership.

Langham Partnership is a global fellowship working in pursuit of the vision God entrusted to its founder John Stott –

> *to facilitate the growth of the church in maturity and Christ-likeness through raising the standards of biblical preaching and teaching.*

Our vision is to see churches in the majority world equipped for mission and growing to maturity in Christ through the ministry of pastors and leaders who believe, teach and live by the Word of God.

Our mission is to strengthen the ministry of the Word of God through:
- nurturing national movements for biblical preaching
- fostering the creation and distribution of evangelical literature
- enhancing evangelical theological education

especially in countries where churches are under-resourced.

Our ministry

Langham Preaching partners with national leaders to nurture indigenous biblical preaching movements for pastors and lay preachers all around the world. With the support of a team of trainers from many countries, a multi-level programme of seminars provides practical training, and is followed by a programme for training local facilitators. Local preachers' groups and national and regional networks ensure continuity and ongoing development, seeking to build vigorous movements committed to Bible exposition.

Langham Literature provides majority world pastors, scholars and seminary libraries with evangelical books and electronic resources through grants, discounts and distribution. The programme also fosters the creation of indigenous evangelical books for pastors in many languages, through training workshops for writers and editors, sponsored writing, translation, strengthening local evangelical publishing houses, and investment in major regional literature projects, such as one volume Bible commentaries like *The Africa Bible Commentary*.

Langham Scholars provides financial support for evangelical doctoral students from the majority world so that, when they return home, they may train pastors and other Christian leaders with sound, biblical and theological teaching. This programme equips those who equip others. Langham Scholars also works in partnership with majority world seminaries in strengthening evangelical theological education. A growing number of Langham Scholars study in high quality doctoral programmes in the majority world itself. As well as teaching the next generation of pastors, graduated Langham Scholars exercise significant influence through their writing and leadership.

To learn more about Langham Partnership and the work we do visit **langham.org**

CPSIA information can be obtained
at www.ICGtesting.com
Printed in the USA
BVHW040032170222
629245BV00004B/444

9 781783 689378